Jewish poems

and

short stories

by

Elliot M. Rubin

cover by David Holifield at Unsplash.com

Dedication
To my grandchildren
Shane, Isabelle, Jonathan, Carter,
Alexandra, Melanie, Mollie, and Madison

In memory of my father
Herman S. Rubin
who wrote poetry and prayers

Preface
This book of Jewish based poems and short stories have all been published before, but are now gathered into one complete collecdtion for your enjoyment.

Table of Contents

the sound of the shofar

the shofar rings out
rushing memories
to my consciousness

i remember as
a child going with
my father to shul,
sitting on his lap
next to my Zayde,
packed in like sardines

looking to my right
i see a black cloth
hung on a white lattice
shielding my Bubbe,
who is sitting with
only women, praying,
i walk around to
visit with her, greeted
with warm hugs and kisses

hearing the blast of the ram's horn
brings back times and people long gone-
with tears of sadness
dripping down my cheeks
the warmth of love
still resonates decades later

listen to the shofar
listen to your heart
listen to their voices
they are still here

Erev Hanukkah

Twas erve Hanukkah,
throughout the whole house,
Mom's brisket was cooking
permeating her blouse

the latkes were sizzling
our home smelled of oil,
we were shvitzing and tired
while the chickens did boil

there was no brick chimney
or old socks to fill,
the kinder sat motionless
by a cold windowsill

waiting for our Bubbe
to visit that night,
and Zayde to drive her
and then have a bite;
of Momma's home cooking,
egg noodles too,
with stuffed derma tummies
we were a full crew

then Uncle Moishe
parked his old battered van,
and out came our cousins
chalk-white with no tan

there are Yossie and Malka,
and Chaim with old Tante Fran,
then Channa, and Dovid,
with Schmuie and some unknown man

he was tall and all wrinkled
with hair flaxen white,
his beard was so long
it seemed not to end

he stepped out
    but needed to bend,
then we saw fall
from his black woolen coat,
some letters and cards
we wrote and did send

to a Rebbe some questions,
just questions, to no end.
but he thought them good,
maybe, that will depend

so everyone did come
for dinner that night;
the Rebbe, the family,
the cousins, you see,
for on erev Hanukkah
there is no TV

the family came
not just for the food,
but to gather together
to joyously schmooze

chocolate challah

the softness is sensual
  sweet to the taste,
    the braids are for gripping
      it's chocolate addictive
hand-rolled and baked
  waiting to be savored,
    the chocolate embedded
      then melted in dough
one bite will tell you
  two will convince,
    the third is orgasmic
      you can't eat enough
they call it chocolate challah
  it's manna from heaven,
    this bet you will win
      it's better than cake!
no butter is needed
  or grape jelly too,
    everyone will love it
      and definitely you

lithuania

in this small baltic nation
there once was a forest
in and near vilnius
of sixty thousand jewish trees
whose roots were hundreds of centuries deep
birthing a bloom of intellect,
poetry, literature, and learning
that spread to every continent—
although almost every tree is cut down,
burned, buried, and chopped to pieces
their roots are deep
their branches spread
the trees are reborn
elsewhere in the world
and they flourish again

understanding

help me understand God;
things happen
which make no sense to me
nor to many others,
if you believe there is a God

help me understand God;
so many genocides took place
in history books, i don't
have enough fingers and toes
to count them all

help me understand God;
though terrible evil happens
people still believe
there is a merciful God,
who looks out for all

help me understand God;
all soldiers in war will tell you
God is in every foxhole,
yet is always on both sides
with youth dying in combat

help me understand God;
why do young children die,
innocents all, some stricken
with the worst diseases
or deformities possible?

help me understand God;
we attribute good things
occurring to a heavenly
guide, yet we don't know
why wickedness exists

help me understand God;
we have free choice, yet
everything is preordained.
is the belief a comfort to our
mind when our end finally comes?

help me understand God!

Belief

The wind can blow and fell a tree,
   It swoops down and removes my hat,
My face turns red from a gusty chill,
   I can't see it, but I know it's there.

when I look into my grandchild's face,
   My heart beats just a little bit faster,
Without touching it, my body feels
   Love exists, yet I cannot see it.

There are some things we feel,
   There are some things we do not see,
There are some things we do not understand,
   Yet, we know they do exist.

Saturday Night Dinner in Brooklyn

The last two slices of rye bread,
Sitting high above the machine,
Are taken by another customer
Who ordered a corned beef on rye

The clerk had no choice,
He had to fill his order,
I need to change my mind
On what to put my dinner

Freshly sliced pumpernickel is tasty,
But I like it in the morning,
Warmed and buttered, with a
Cup of hot chocolate and a little swirl of cream

I ask if there is any club bread left,
In a pinch, I've had it too,
But fresh sliced Jewish rye bread,
Is my preference, how about you?

My face showed disappointment,
So the clerk cut me a schtickle,
While he piled the corned beef high,
With mustard and a pickle

The sandwich is wrapped in wax paper,
A sour pickle slipped between the crease,
And a Doctor Brown's Black Cherry soda
He placed in the bag with ease

There are few kosher delis,
Where once there were too many,
Assimilation killed them off, I know,
Thank God, a few are left

Herman the Hanukkah Candle

Herman the Hanukkah Candle
  Has a very shiny flame,
And if you ever saw it,
  You would even say the same

All of the other candles,
  Used to laugh and call him names,
They never let poor Herman,
  Play in any dreidle games

Then one misty Hanukkah night,
  The Rebbi came to say,
"Herman, with your flame so bright,
  Won't you light the menorah tonight?"

Then all the candles loved him,
  As they dovened out with glee,
Herman the Hanukkah Candle,
  You'll go down in history!

a walk in isolation

my knee felt good this morning
the arthritis is sleeping,
i'm pain-free–
looking out
i see the slight misty rain
has stopped
leaving a sheen of gloss
on black asphalt streets–
putting on sneakers
i start the first
of my three daily walks.
as the road twists and turns
i am alone
this early morning;
i begin to think of
my bar mitzvah 61 years ago–
the chazon opens the curtain
of the Aron Chodesh
lifts a Torah out, places
it on the table–
he unrolls to the day's portion
calls up to the bemah
two readers
when it is my turn
i start to recite three required prayers
when i look out
at the filled sanctuary
spotting my grandfather
sitting with my parents–
tears are streaming down his face
as i carry on the tradition
of the family heleft behind
years ago in Europe;
remembering those slaughtered
in the woods by Nazis–
a car wakes me
from my thoughts
as i step to the side,
letting both the vehicle
and my thoughts pass along

old myron schwartz and angel sanchez

born in poverty to a homeless mom
they were found wandering streets
by an elderly, lonely man
who took them in
fed them with meats and sweets
the seven-year-old boy
calls him father
years of love
never a bother, kindness
was the only house rule
old myron schwartz took him
to baseball games
played catch till dusk
bought him a bat, ball, and glove
often fished together by a stream

one day old myron schwartz stayed in bed
he could only move his head
the young boy wept and held his hand
and did not move, not one inch
 poppa i love you, please don't go
momma and i still need you so
the old man strains his arm
grips the boy's hand
      i give you my blessing, everything i own
      i love you.
then took his last breath
a life of empathy
remembered after death

A Talmudic discussion

A week ago, a group of Rubinic (not Rabbinic) scholars debated the use of straws.

It started with the traditional premise that one cannot drink a glass of milk if eating meat.

The Food and Drug Administration signaled plans to start enforcing a federal standard that defines "milk" as coming from the "milking of one or more healthy cows." Jul 18, 2018 (this is a fact, really)

A well-versed Rubinic scholar stated a straw goes from the glass of milk into the mouth. The milk does not touch a person's lips, thereby constituting one is not drinking milk but sucking. Thus, the prohibition (of drinking) is bypassed as the fluid goes directly into the digestive process keeping the lips dry. This turns out to be the Rubinic majority viewpoint.

According to the FDA, another Rubinic scholar likened it to an infant drinking/straw-like sucking breastmilk, not classified as milk. He was in the minority.

A younger Rubinic scholar brought up the composition of the straw. It is not allowed if it is from genetic material such as paper. Plastic, though, will be allowed. The majority agreed.

Also, if it is chocolate milk, and the milk is less than 1/60th of the contents, you are allowed to drink it without a straw!

I hope this clarifies everything.

my Zayde

My Bubbe bought me a toy drum,
The dog heard it and then would come
My family drank wine, never demon rum,
and most of them are very frum

I loved playing with my brand-new toy
Except for my Zayde, who seems like a goy
My mishbucha never said a word
About what they all knew or heard

It seems momma had secrets to keep,
No rumors from her mouth would seep,
They all were able to speak some Yiddish,
Except for Zayde, who came for the kiddish

The secret language he did not speak
So all the family thought him a freak,
But he loved me with all his heart,
And worldly knowledge he would impart

He'd go out to eat pork fried rice
Then drink years-old whiskey   on ice,
He'd run home to shower for Shabbat
Before Bubbe would kiss him a lot

The rabbi's sermon would bring on a yawn
He'd doze off, then wake before dawn-
No pills to sleep or meditate on
A few shots at night, and he was long gone

The Obligation

My grandmother was married to a self-centered, stubborn, yet financially successful man who was my grandfather.

Born in Polish Austria, my grandmother's birth certificate had her mother's maiden name and not her father's. Her parents were married by a rabbi, but back in the 1800's Europe, if you were not married in the church, your children were considered illegitimate; thus, her mother's maiden name.

Like her mother, who came from a well-to-do family, she was homeschooled by a tutor, unlike other Jewish girls who were not given an academic education. Her mother died when my grandmother was fifteen (I do not know how her father was predeceased), and as the oldest child, her mother, on her deathbed, made my grandmother promise to care for her two younger sisters and brother; keeping them together and seeing they married a Jewish spouse.

After her mother's passing, an aunt took in the three girls but did not want to raise a boy, so she placed my grandmother's young brother Julian in a boys orphanage. Trying to keep a promise to her mother, she somehow became engaged to a man in America. This gentleman promised if she married him, he would pay to bring over her siblings.

When she arrived in New York and settled in Brooklyn, her fiancé reneged on the deal and said he would not bring over the rest of her family. Immediately she ended the engagement.

Luckily her former fiancé had a friend (my grandfather) who I was told had his eye on her, and after the engagement ended, said he would bring her siblings to America if she married him. So they married, and he kept his word.

As he became more successful, he built a building for his business, and on top was an eight-room apartment for his family.

Besides her three siblings, my grandmother gave birth to two sons and a daughter with my grandfather in their home. They were all living in the same house. This was not a marriage of love and romance but one of obligation.

As all the children grew up, eventually, they moved out of the house.

One sister was employed as a housekeeper for a wealthy Italian family in California and moved there. When her employer impregnated her, my grandmother arranged for her to marry a Jewish cabinetmaker back in Brooklyn. She moved back to Brooklyn, had the baby, and the child bore her husband's last name.

The youngest sister eloped and married her Italian supervisor from the laundry where she worked. This caused a split in the family, which lasted almost 100 years.

Grandma's kid brother, who also spoke German/Yiddish, joined the American army and was sent back to Europe to fight during World War One and survived. After the war, he had strict orders not to be buried for three days after his passing to make sure he was dead. In the trenches of the war, he saw men buried alive.

In the hot and humid summer months in New York City, my grandfather would go to the Catskills for a vacation, but he never took my grandmother or any of the kids along with him. He enjoyed the cool mountain summers while she cooked, cleaned, and raised their children as well as her siblings before there was air conditioning, without complaining.

Once all the kids moved out, only her daughter, my mother, was left at home.

My grandfather closed off the back rooms of the apartment and made it into a separate apartment he rented to a Jewish widower and his two twenty-something sons. The young men were going to St. Johns University at night during the great depression, and one of them was to be my father. But my mother was already engaged to someone else when they moved in.

Grandma was not overly fond of my mother's fiancé but liked my father and preferred she marry him instead. So every time she saw him in the hallway, dad was invited in for coffee and cake or a cookie. My mother used to say he was always in the kitchen noshing with her mother.

Eventually, she broke off the engagement and married my father. Grandma won out.

My mother was now married; my grandfather felt she was now her husband's responsibility, no longer his.

His oldest son eloped and married a Jewish girl whose mother was an atheist and anarchist. This was reason enough not to send him to medical school as he desired. It was a punishment, but he brought him into an auto parts business he owned.

The younger son was a car mechanic barely making a living; he was the favored son.

To help his boys, Grandpa had started a scrap metal business. Today their sons, my first cousins, do very well. One drives a Bentley and lives on the water on the Long Island Sound with tennis courts and an in-ground saltwater pool. My other cousin retired at forty to Key West and has since died. I officiated his funeral.

My grandfather had a severe heart attack in his sixties, and the doctor said he should go to Florida and recuperate.

Remembering the years when he vacationed in the Catskill Mountains and left her with the children in the city to sweat, grandma refused to go with him. My mother spoke to her regarding her father's health, and grandma said she would only go if my grandfather took my mother and her whole family. So that year, my sister, parents, and I flew to Miami Beach with my grandparents. We spent weeks swimming and sightseeing around the South Florida- Miami area.

There is usually a special bond between a mother and a daughter. My grandmother fulfilled her obligation to her dying mother as best she could; she lived in a loveless marriage, trying to keep that promise.

closed

when a synagogue closes
it is worse than a tragedy
it is a death
not a single death, but the
death of a jewish community

on the high holidays
when the shofar sounds
the ghosts
of those who prayed there rise
to remember the simchas
and the memorial kaddish
many recited over the years

the building is now empty,
sometimes torn down
sometimes used for other purposes
yet in the memories of past members
it still lives on

the midnight ride of Paulie Reverowitz

Paulie, slow down, you'll choke on the knadels, the horse can wait, Momma said.

Momma, I need to warn the shtetls that the red-coated Cossacks are coming. Moishe climbed the shul's steps to the steeple and flashed two triple A flashlights. He could have gotten a heart attack, God forbid, from those farbissena steps.

Why not take poppas horse, he's older and slower. You won't fall off.

No time, I must leave now before they get to Lexington and Concord.

Here, put on your heavy sweater, I don't want you should get a chill, and your wool scarf too, the one Tante Goldie made for you.

*Momma, please, **I have to go.***

Ok ok, here, I wrapped a pastrami sandwich for you. Put it in the red flaishic saddle bag. The yellow one is milichdic. Don't mix them up, or I'll have to re-kosher them. Your Zaidi did that once, may his memory be a blessing.

I remember I remember. You never let him forget it. Love you, momma, have to go.

WAIT! That's how you dress? Your boots need a shine. Do you want the neighbors to talk about you? You want them to say Mable Reverowitz can't afford to buy her son new boots. A shanda.

It's dark out, momma, nobody will see my boots.

So, nobody will come out to look at the crazy man shouting something about Cossacks coming and riding on a horse? I would. Here, put on these clean ones.

No time momma, I really have to go.

At least take the Turnpike Trail. They have rest stops, just in case.

morals

i try to live my life
doing the right thing–
the views i hold are shared
only with like-minded friends,
never trying to impose
my values or morals on others
as vines do to trees;
smothering them,
taking their life force,
their individuality,
until the tree dies
not realizing
they, too, will die

the tombstone observed

you see a reminder of someone's life
written in a language long thought dead,
but alive in small communities worldwide
telling of a woman's last request

it explains to strangers she has no family,
no one left to remember her
begging anyone who reads this stone
to say a memorial prayer for a lonely woman

the people who read it
understand her request–
every year, a candle is lit, and
a prayer said for her long lost memory

conflicted hate

i hate you, although we never met–
when i see where you are   or came from
i delete your words
i delete your thoughts
i delete you completely
before you even can tell me
what you want to say

it is a visceral feeling
rooted in my childhood
hearing of the holocaust,
young relatives, i never met
yet saw pictures of
before their dreary slow march
into the dark shadowed woods of death

i'd rather embrace you,
love you, but your leaders swear
to kill all my kind, to push them
into the sea–
they are of my bloodline,
you are of my bloodline,
this madness must stop

the hate must be buried
with both of our dead loved ones
for this madness   to end in peace

details

i stand in the rear
of every religious service
i attend
      watching
as the congregation
prays in unison
looking down at a book
hoping their prayers go up

the ceiling, i think,
blocks their calls of mercy,
their wishes for others
or for something to help with

too often, their god doesn't respond

when requests are answered
i wonder if it's a coincidence
or divine intervention,
      maybe
someday i'll find out,
but by then
      how can i tell you

Irving the Litvak

he was a typical old-time
New York cabby
wearing a newsboy cap,
always two days of unshaved stubble
on his face with three inches
left on a chewed cigar
dangling from his lips,
speaking with a gravelly voice
is how he is remembered

he was my uncle's brother-in-law.

since my uncle didn't drive
he drove him around
to visit his sister, my grandmother

the Litvak was an older, burned out
city hack driver who years later,
i learned,
charged my uncle a fare
even though it was on a Sunday,
and their wives were
always with them

our encounters never lasted more
then fifteen minutes or so
when my uncle visited;
the Litvak's taxi downstairs
still had the meter running

so much for a warm
congenial,
extended family gathering

visit to the cemetery

on a windy November morning,
a bone-chilling gust slams into me
as i stand on an open field
when i turn my head
to look at an isolated grave

the grey stone monument
tells me her name
and her date of death; she's
an eighteen-month-old girl

her grave stands alone,
not amongst the others
in the packed cemetery;
the rest of the plots
for thirty feet around
are all fallow,
empty, not filled

where are her family
members buried?
she was interred here
seventy years ago,
yet there are no others
keeping her company

she is somebody's daughter,
but whose i may never know;
yet every year i place
a single stone on her grave
and say a prayer,
because somebody
has to remember her

in memoriam

please do not weep for me-
i had a good life,
found love, success, enjoyed
myself as i went along.
luck had a lot to do with it,
some say you make your luck,
i don't know

i laughed a lot,
saw humor where others did not;
developed a crying heart
when sadness and problems
overcame strangers in life

in the end, i know some of you
will shed a tear or two for me,
some will laugh at the things
i said or did in life;
both are acceptable

my final words are
love someone, laugh a lot,
don't forget to be kind, and
charitable; then eat something
i'd enjoy, and share it with others

oh, one more thing-
be a mensch!
my father always
said it me to me;
it helps

to my shaina maidella daughters

don't be
the woman
he wants–
be the woman
you want,
then
if he wants
you,
he will want
you

a walk in isolation

my knee felt good this morning,
arthritis is sleeping, i'm pain-free–
looking out i see the fine misty rain
has stopped, leaving a sheen of gloss
on black asphalt streets
putting on sneakers i start the first
of my three daily walks–
as the road twists and turns
i am alone this early morning;
i start to think of my bar mitzvah 61 years ago–
the Hazon opens the curtain of the Aron Chodesh
lifting a Torah out, placing it on the table–
he unrolls to the day's portion
then calls up to the bemah two readers–
when it's my turn–
i start to recite three required prayers
when i look up at the filled sanctuary,
spotting my grandfather sitting with my parents–
tears are streaming down his face
as i carry on the tradition
of the family, he left behind
years ago in Europe;
remembering those slaughtered
in the woods by Nazis

a car wakes me
from my thoughts
as i step to the side
of the road
letting both the vehicle
and my thoughts pass along

condolences

what do you say
to someone who
lost their spouse
of many years?

there are no words
you can offer
to ease the sorrow
or dry the tears

although the english
language borrows,
then incorporates,
foreign words as their own
it still lacks the right words

how can you console
the inconsolable?

stones

as i walk in life
there are stepping stones
to help me,
as there might be for others

with empathy in my heart
i can't bear
to overturn them,
for fear of what i might find

too much sorrow,
grief and hurt
for one person
to bear in a lifetime

how can i help them
when their agony
so overcomes my
heart- i cry out

at the inhumanity
others suffer; with
little solace or
care afforded them

where is God?

god

where is god?
where can you find god?

when children are crying
ribs sticking out from hunger
illness thirsting for more victims
people living on the streets
families in cardboard boxes
digging through garbage cans
for discarded food

god stands for
charity,
hope,
salvation,
goodness,
empathy,
kindness

inside, we are all god

the problem is
we do not
knowingly
acknowledge
this fact,
or act on it

walk'n and talk'n with god

as i walk down the staircase of life
i'm coming to the final few steps
where i'll end my long tiresome journey;
depression and despair are constant companions
when i hear a gentle voice whispering out to me;
wait and listen, so i did

come walk with me we'll talk a little-
god held my hand i felt so secure;
he gave me the hope i lost long ago;
i listened to words i forgot from my youth

i turned around and walked back up-
god was with me step by step,
never leaving me alone to fall

i walked and talked
a while;
i'm so glad;
i found a way back home

remorse

on the side of my parent's driveway
is a long sliver of grass and trees
with the most massive anthill i ever saw;
as a ten-year-old, i had to destroy it

the tiny creatures were nothing to me,
they had no rights to exist or be there,
so i did everything i could to kill them
but they always rebuilt their mounds

i'm seventy-four and remember it well.
this morning i killed a spider in my home;
i felt such remorse after squashing it
my mind sprang back to sunny days of youth

i am driving down the highway of life,
seeing the dark endless tunnel ahead;
now understanding all life is sacred;
forgive me, for i feel guilt over my past

prayer

i remember the day well
when i realized
i was not
getting anything
out of a religious service

it was about
the middle
when i stood,
then walked out–
it has been
at least ten years
if not more
since i've been back

in biblical times
there were no
organized prayer books
where people recited by rote
words from their mouth
and not from their soul

their heart
spoke to god,
not from
someone else's
words in a book

sabbath question

as i walk by the worship building
on the town square
tower bells ring out,
i look to see if god's angels
are outside
waving me in
to meet,
to talk to,
to see
if i have anything of value to say

does god want to hear my trivia
while there are so many
other worthwhile things
as i watch the sinners walk-in
every week
　　　　　never reforming?

why bother her/him/them on the one day of rest?

momma

i'm old now
over the hill
i feel so alone
without you here
i miss you so much

i want to talk
hold your hand
like we did
years ago
when you walked me
to bed at night

we talked about problems
we talked about good times
we talked about everything
who can i talk to now
i'm facing the end soon

intellect

there once were three wise men in Chelm
whose intellect would surely overwhelm
the most brilliant men in the realm
a rowboat they could not even helm

if one were to ask their advice
you'd need to ask it twice
although they are very nice
their answers are like playing dice

grandma

she entered a marriage of necessity
not one of love
the person i adored
overflowed with it

a mother's deathbed request
see my children marry jewish–
after death
bessie, etta, and frances
lived with an aunt,
julian, the brother, went to an orphanage

a stranger brought grandma to america
to marry, *only if my siblings come too–*
once here, he reneged to bring them

his friend said he would do it–
that man became my grandfather,
emotionally shallow, with
cold business instincts–
he kept his word,

she tried to keep her promise to her mother

sat shiva when the baby sister
eloped with a non-jew

never knew the sister existed till i was past forty–
i healed the rift after ninety years had passed

value

we all are born
    with nothing
we all leave
    with nothing

the values
    we leave behind
are the deeds we did
    which people remember

ordained

ungodly men of god

sinners of lust and avarice

different faiths

same faults

poisoned fruits

they mouth holy words

speak of holy deeds

as their flock blindly follows

while satan and lillith laugh

at this foolhardy folly

undertakers

they drive luxury sedans

always colored in heartbroken black

when called, they arrive

with sad dower looks

they park the hearse

then go inside

to soon come out

with a closed black bag

and inside is a hidden, cold corpse

to be prepared for its final interment

it's a career comprised

of grief and compassion, you see,

not a jovial job for faint of heart

eventually   they will come for me

finding someone

kasper kaputsky sought love

hopefully long term

but tonight, is good too

he tried eharmony,

bumble, and

tinder also, to look for her

caitlin catalina caught

his eye, he swiped right

tried to meet her

she answered back

not interested at all,

his heart went kaputsky

his voice in my mind

i can hear
my father's voice
as he gives me
heartfelt advice
based on life experience,
and the 1930s depression
which greatly influenced his views–
be cautious,
think everything through
then make your decision, plus
a myriad
of other sage sayings
i've heard and filed in my mind
to bring back before
i went forward–
i knew
he had my back if i fell
i knew
he would always be in my life
as i went forward
until his aneurysm 35 years ago

why god cries

god's tears
are torrents
            on a sunny day
while sadness reigns
and innocents die

man is given choice
too often, the wrong one,
yet fails to learn from it
and god cries

often

My Mother's Voice

Kids are asleep, my wife is upstairs,
  Late news is over, the lights are turned down.
Silence is comforting as I think of my life,
  When in my ear, my mother speaks softly to me

The past just then roars back to my youth,
  Protected from harm and smothered with love.
Not a care in the world, and my future ahead,
  I smile, lay back, and welcome the past

My mother is sitting and stroking my head,
  Grandma is ironing my sheets, so I'm warm,
A cold wind is blowing, and it's freezing outside,
  But I'm sleepy and cuddled and ready for bed

Goodnight my love I'll see you tomorrow,
  I'll take you to school and bake you a treat,
I remember her voice as clear as a bell,
  My eyes swell up with tears streaming down

Every time I hear my mother's sweet voice,
  My heart aches and hurts I miss her so much,
Into my ears, she whispers so often,
  It's as if she'll never leave me alone

The Rabbi

The Rabbi would never eat pork. It was not kosher and it was forbidden for him to eat.

In his whole life he had never even touched anything from a pig, let alone eat it.

He was a young rabbi in his late thirties and was single. He had studied in Israel as well as the rabbinical colleges in America.

Now he was hired for a new synagogue with a mostly young congregation. It was his first congregation and he really wanted to do well.

The older women in the congregation started to talk to him about their nieces and granddaughters. A marriage with the rabbi wouldn't be so bad. Actually they thought it would be great as he was young, educated and had a wholesome look about him.

He wasn't a bad-looking fellow. Kind of thin, wore glasses, and was very friendly and soft-spoken.

On Tuesdays, his day off, he would go to the bookstore to see what new books had come in. As was his custom, he would buy a book, walk to the coffee shop in the bookstore, and read while sipping his coffee.

Then one day a young woman came into the crowded coffee shop and asked if he would mind if she sat down at his small table as there were no other empty seats available.

Her eyes were light blue and they glowed against her dark brown hair. They call this combination an "American beauty." They were riveting when you looked into them. They were almost like the blue steely eyes of a forest wolf staring at you down his muzzle. It was very hypnotizing.

The rabbi said it was alright to sit with him. There was plenty of space at his table.

Her perfume wafted through the coffee aroma and swept toward the rabbi's face. He smelled her before he saw her.

Then he looked up and looked right into her face.

The most beautiful face he had ever seen. Only God could make a face like this, he thought to himself.

In the earliest days of creation in order for the species to continue they had to mate. To help things along hormones came into play. Thousands of years later they still exist and are for the most part uncontrollable.

It doesn't matter what your upbringing, or how you were raised. When a boy's eyes meet the right girl's eyes, their hormones begin to do what they were meant to do.

When the rabbi looked in the eyes of this most beautiful of women his hormones started to act up. How could he speak to her and not act foolish? He spoke to his congregation every Saturday and was not tongue tied like he was now. What is happening?

The young woman sat down and crossed her legs, with her red plaid skirt settling just above her knees. The gold cross she was wearing was glistening as were her red polished shoes that matched the color of her fingernails. So perfect, so put together.

"Hi," she said, introducing herself. "Do you come here often?" she asked.

The rabbi's mind started to race. She is not Jewish, she probably eats pork products. What if we start talking and find out we like each other? She is so beautiful. What if something develops and we go out on a date? Is it okay to kiss non-kosher lips? What a predicament he was in.

Maybe they could meet next Tuesday also, he thought. But he never ushered the words.

It was not to be.

Moses

After forty years of wandering in the desert the People of Israel were on the precipice of entering the Promised Land.

They were tired of schlepping around and going nowhere. So they gathered together one day and pleaded with Heaven. "Please speak to Moses. We have been traipsing through the desert for forty years. It's very hot, the scenery is nothing to speak of, and the sand gets between our toes and is irritating to our skin."

"We know that you can do this for us. You are the only one in heaven and there are no others. And we have always kept you in the forefront of our minds and in our hearts. Plus we have written this pledge on the entrance to every one of our tents."

"If you could see it in your heart to take pity on us and speak to Moses we pledge to tell our children of your miracles, and they their children."

Heaven then sent an angel to speak to Moses. The angel found him sitting on a ledge overlooking the valley below that was in the Promised Land.

"Moishe, Vas Mackster? [What's up] the angel asked in Yiddish.

"Vouse es doose" [what is this?] Moses replied. "I don't know how but we are speaking in a strange language that I never learned" said Moses.

The angel told him that Heaven wanted him to see the future. That would be one of the hundreds of languages his chosen people will speak.

They will be scattered all over the Earth teaching his commandments and trying to make the world a better place to live. Moses looked out at the great expanse and then saw Mom-a-lers making kreplach, sweet and sour stuffed cabbage, and also potato knishes.

He saw young Hebrew children reading Torah and studying Heaven's laws. But Moses was not satisfied.

"Listen" he said to the angel, "I have so much more to teach them. Let me take one more meander in the desert. During the forty years I led them, I wore out 613 pairs of sandals. With each sandal I would instruct the people in another commandment[1]."

"Moses" the angel replied, "we must leave the rest for the future to figure out. You have given them the basis of Heaven's laws, now the people will have to use their brains to finish the job".

The angel said that if Moses could buy a new pair of sandals he could go out one more time.

Moses then went to the tent of Itzick Bloomingdale, the clothier, to buy a new pair of sandals. But he was sold out. The same thing happened when he went to see Sollie Lauren and his camel etched sandals.

With a deep breath he had no choice but to spend a lot to get a new pair of sandals. He had to go to the designer tent of Manny Manulo Levi. But alas, he too was sold out. But he did have a thick blue fabric for a new pair of pants.

So the angel made a face saving deal with Moses because Heaven favored Moses.

If Moses would instruct the People of Israel to pray every morning and evening, that there was only One in heaven and there were no others, Heaven would allow them into the Promised Land and stop the drifting around. As a bonus heaven would make it rain in the proper season, they will be fruitful, and multiply like the stars in sky.

So Moses did as he was asked and the People of Israel entered the Promised Land.

---

[1] In the Jewish faith there are 613 commandments that an observant person is to do every day. It covers from the time they wake up till they go to sleep.

A MEMORIA SH'MA

A Memorial Sh'ma。

Chazan & Congregartion	Leader
Sh'ma -	I hear the trains arriving and screeching to a halt
Yis-ra-eil, -	I see the mass of my people herded, waiting for selection.
A-do-nai –	I believe God will take their souls to his bosom
E-lo-hei-nu, -	I know God is my master, not anyone else
A-do-nai –	I acknowledge that God will see me through my problems
E-chad. –	I believe He is the only one that can.

Thank you for reading my book, it is appreciated.

Please check out my website for other books I have written.

www.CreativeFiction.net

My Instagranm Account is elliot_m_rubin

www.ingramcontent.com/pod-product-compliance
Lightning Source LLC
Chambersburg PA
CBHW070031110426
42741CB00035B/2722